JACK THE RIPPER

-

Tour Managua

English

Thomas Hattemer

JACK THE RIPPER

-

Tour Managua

Code in Carl Feigenbaum,
Photo 1892

English

FSC
www.fsc.org
MIX
Papier aus ver-
antwortungsvollen
Quellen
Paper from
responsible sources
FSC® C105338

Bibliografische Information der Deutschen Nationalbibliothek
Die Deutsche Nationalbibliothek verzeichnet diese Publikation
in der Deutschen Nationalbibliografie; detaillierte bibliografische
Daten sind im Internet über http://dnb.d-nb.de abrufbar.

© 2022 Thomas Hattemer Covergestaltung,
Herstellung und Verlag: BoD - Books on Demand,
Norderstedt
Grafik: PixieMe/ BigAlBaloo/ Ografica/ Danler/
Shutterstock.com
ISBN 978-3-7562-4957-2

Table of contents

Jacob Köth III. (1850 - 1904), builder of the 1888 house in Pfaffen-Schwabenheim. Probably link between two serial killers (Horrweiler, Gau-Bickelheim) and the noble clients. Because of the distances from the 1888 house to London, Koblenz and Frankfurt and the same angles in London and Rheinhessen (93.82), his death "out of town" in the month of Herbert von Bismarck's death, etc., probably involved in the action.

Managua – January 1889 – 6 Murders

Similar to Jack the Ripper

In January 1889, six prostitutes are murdered in Managua, the capital of Nicaragua.
The murders take place in less than ten days.
The murderer disappears without a trace.

Some newspapers at the time raise the question whether this might not be the same murderer who officially killed five women in London (Whitechapel and Spitalfields districts) in the autumn of 1888:

Jack the Ripper

There are only the newspaper articles of the time. Original sources on the operation at the local police station were destroyed in the 1931 and 1972 earthquakes. This is how the editor of a local newspaper in Managua, Archimedes Gonzales, reported it to ex-detective and researcher Trevor Marriott in England. [1]

I asked myself, if the number six wants to tell us something.

Same Killer: 4x London and 6x Managua

Based on the codes in distances (London and Managua) angles (London) and names of persons and streets (London)

---

[1] Marriott, Trevor: Jack the Ripper, The 21th Century Investigation

I can show that the following murders were committed by the same person Anton Zahn:

1. Mary Ann Nichols (1845 – Aug. 31, 1888)
2. Annie Chapman (1841 – Sept. 8, 1888)
3. Elizabeth Stride (1843 – Sept. 30, 1888)
4. Catherine Eddowes (1842 – Sept. 30, 1888)
5. – 10. Six prostitutes in Managua (mid-January 1889)

In my book before, I showed that a German order from the very top may be behind this, which historians and others should re-examine.

Mary Jane Kelly killed without order

The following murder, in my opinion, does not fit into the pattern I had found out for London in 2021; reason: I cannot determine any coding.
Therefore I suspect that it could have been a copycat. Or: Jack the Ripper or Anton Zahn alias Carl Feigenbaum did it himself, but only "privately", i.e. without instructions from above.

Mary Jane Kelly (ca. 1863 - Nov. 9, 1888)

After all, this murder is 5 weeks after the last two murders. All the others are no more than 3 weeks apart.

In the other killings Aug. 31 – Sept. 30, 1888, and January 1889, numerous codings can be discerned. This was long planned in detail from above.

Just as the number 4 in London (with the slightly crooked cross) says something, the number 6 in Managua does.

The Star, Guernsey reports

Otherwise enable them to do.

"JACK THE RIPPER" IN CENTRAL AMERICA.

SIX WOMEN MURDERED AND MUTILATED.

The New York *Sun*, of the 6th inst., publishes the following special dispatch from Managua, Nicaragua, dated the 24th of January :—

THE VICTIMS.

Either Jack the Ripper, of Whitechapel, has emigrated from the scene of his ghastly murders or he has found one or more imitators in this part of Central America. The people have been greatly aroused by six of the most atrocious murders ever committed within the limits of this city. The murderer or murderers have vanished as quickly as Jack the Ripper, and no traces have been left for identification. All of the victims were women of the character of those who met their fate at the hands of the London murderer. Like those women of Whitechapel, they were women who had sank to the lowest degradations of their calling. They have been found murdered just as mysteriously, and the murders point to almost identical methods. Two were found butchered out of all recognition. Even their faces were most horribly slashed, and in the cases of all the others their persons were frightfully disfigured.

ROBBERY NOT THE MURDERER'S OBJECT.

Like "Jack the Ripper's" victims, they have been found in out-of-the-way places, three of them in the suburbs of the town, and the others in dark alleys and corners. Two of the victims were found with gaudy jewellery, and from this it is urged that the mysterious murderer has not committed the crimes for robbery. In the cases of the other four a few coins were found on their persons, representing no doubt the prospective consideration for the murderer or murderers. All of the victims were in the last stages of shabbiness and besottedness. In fact in almost every detail the crimes and the characteristics are identical with the Whitechapel horrors. All the murders occurred in less than ten days, and as yet the perpetrator or perpetrators have not been apprehended. Every effort is being made to bring him or them to justice. The authorities have been stimulated in their efforts by the statement, which seems to be generally accepted, that Jack the Ripper must have emigrated to Central America and selected this city for his temporary abode.

2

" "'Jack the Ripper' in Central America", The Star, Saint Peter Port, Guernsey, Eng. 21 Feb. 1889

---

2 https://www.newspapers.com/clip/26108101/jack-the-ripper-in-central/

Codes in Managua – like London

London – Rhinehesse: 600 km, from there 6, 60 km

In my book "Jack the Ripper - Deutscher vom Rhein" (Jack the Ripper - German from the Rhine) I had stated that the distance from the point of intersection of the first four murders in London (31.8.-30.9.1888) to Anton Zahn's (alias Carl Feigenbaum) birthplace Gau-Bickelheim is 600 kilometres. 200 metres east of the cemetery is the point.

Exactly from this point in Gau-Bickelheim to the 1888 house in Pfaffen-Schwabenheim is 6 kilometres.

From the 1888 house to the middle of the Krönungsweg in Frankfurt between the cathedral and the Römer and to the southern end of the Kaiserin-Augusta-Anlagen in Koblenz is exactly 60 kilometres in each case.

So 600, 60, 6.

In my book in 2021 I had stated that "Jack the Ripper" is, in my opinion, "Anton Zahn alias Carl Feigenbaum". And: He acts on behalf.

So I would like to know, if traces of the murderer also can be found in Central America, and: intentionally laid tracks.

Despite the earthquake there still remain for the investigation:

a) The word "Agua" in Managua and Nicaragua,
b) the history of the country at that time,
c) the number six.

What lies 6, 60, 600 or even 6000 km away from Managua?
Where exactly in Managua is the starting point?

The places where the murdered women were deposited can no longer be traced. And perhaps they don't have to be.

The press wrote at the time:
3 women were found in suburbs, 3 others on avenues in the city centre.

Which traces should be laid?

a) Spanish element (next to English). I am thinking of „Carlos / Charles Feigenbaum", so that codes are created from it, which provide further clues to Anton Zahn alias Carl Feigenbaum.
b) As in London, a revenge of the German Reich?
c) Statement: "If you find the 6, 60, 600 km from Managua, then see if it is not also 600 km from London to the killer's place of origin!"

Nothing can be coded in street names as it is in London. Managua, like Manhattan, has numbered names, unlike Havana, for example, the capital in Cuba.

At first I tried to find smooth distances to other cities (!) in Nicaragua or to those abroad. But no suitable distance could be found that would have been exactly 60 or 600 km. So water remains.

Spanish word for "water" in city and state

Maybe you are not supposed to connect cities ... That is what the name of Managua points to. So I have to find a "water" and see what waters can be found from there in 6, 60, 600 and maybe even 6000 km.

The English-language Wikipedia page on Managua says:

<< There are two possible origins for the name "Managua". It could come from the term Mana-ahuac, which translates as "beside the water" or "surrounded by water" in the indigenous Nahuatl language. Or it may come from the Mangue language, where the word Managua means "place of the great man" or "chief." >> [3]

... And about the country Nicaragua it says:

<< There are two prevailing theories about how the name "Nicaragua" came to be. The first is that the name was coined by Spanish colonists, based on the name Nicarao, who was the chief or cacique of a powerful indigenous tribe encountered by the Spanish conquistador Gil González Dávila when he entered southwestern Nicaragua in 1522. This theory claims that the name Nicaragua was formed from Nicarao and agua (Spanish for "water") to refer to the fact that there are two large lakes and several other bodies of water in the country. As of 2002, however, it was established that the real name of the cacique was Macuilmiquiztli, which means "five deaths" in the Nahuatl language, and not Nicarao. The second theory is that the name of the country comes from one of the following Nahuatl words: nic-anahuac, meaning "Anahuac has come this far" or "the Nahuas have come this far" or "those who come from Anahuac have come this far" ; nican-nahua, meaning "here are the Nahuas"; or nic-atl-nahuac, meaning "here by the water" or "surrounded by water." >> [4]

---

[3] https://en.wikipedia.org/wiki/Managua
[4] https://en.wikipedia.org/wiki/Nicaragua

Waters 6, 60, 600, 6000 km from Laguna de Tiscapa

The only question is which lake, which pond, to take as a starting point for sixes distances.
There is the big lake on which Managua is situated, and there are ponds within the city or on what was then the outskirts.

Where do I get a striking distance?

Central to Managua is the pond „Laguna de Tiscapa".
This is exactly our starting point.
It is located about 2.3 km south of the lake "Lago Xolotian", to which Managua nestles.

If you go 60 km south from Tiscapa, you reach the sea coast at the Pacific, more precisely at 61.5 km. (60 km: slightly tilted to the west).

But that is the indication that bodies of water are meant!

As an aside: The „Refugio de Vida Silvestre Río Escalante Chacocente" is located where the crow flies reaches the Pacific Ocean at about 60 km further south,

At a pond "Lago de Asasosca" to the west of the city, it is about 58 km south to the Pacific Ocean.

Let's continue:
What do you meet as the crow flies at 6 and 600 km?
- At a distance of 6 km, one reaches the "Laguna de Nejapa" west-southwest on the outskirts of the city. From the centre of the "Laguna de Tiscapa" to the centre of the "Laguna de Nejapa" it is 5.92 kilometres. In the southwest corner of the

pond (southern two-fifths) you still have water under your feet at a distance of 6 km.
- At a distance of 600 km, one meets the lake "Lago de Atilan" in the northern state of Guatemala. More precisely: the middle of the eastern half of the lake.

Motive „Knife" 2x in 6000 km Distance

But it gets even crazier, because the word "knife" seems to be hidden 6000 km to the north <u>and</u> 6000 km to the south:

- 6000 km to the north, you meet the "Great Slave Lake" in Canada. More precisely: a bay in the north. At a distance of 6024 km from Managua lies the city of Yellowknife. The city was founded in 1930, but the people there have lived there for a very long time, at least since before 1889.

- South of Managua in Argentina, after 6000 km, you reach 6 lakes that stand in a row. From space, they look like a knife blade tapering to a point. "Laguna Alsina" is the largest lake. Amazing, because the lakes have a width of only 3, 5 and 8 km respectively. The two western lakes are reached exactly, the others at 6001 to 6003 km.

Is it coincidence, or is the word "knife" meant to be referred to in the 6000 km distance; once in the form of the "Yellowknife" people in Canada and once in the form of the lakes in Argentina?

1888 Metres from Cathedral to Laguna de Tiscapa

Amazing: Approx. 1888 or 1889 <u>metres</u> south of the big old "Catedral Santiago Apostol", which has been a ruin since the earthquake in 1972, the centre of the pond "Laguna de Tiscapa" is hit! (Or at least to within about 25 metres). The cathedral was not built until 1925. However, there was a predecessor building.

On the Spanish Wikipedia it says:
<< The oldest church was the Parroquia, which stood exactly where the old cathedral is today. This temple was in ruins, so Presbyter Juan Antonio Chamorro Guatemala asked permission to demolish and rebuild it. In 1781, the colonial church fell. When five years passed and nothing was solved, the priest Chamorro covered the cost and, with the labour of the indigenous people of Tipitapa, built the foundations, which cost him 1,178 silver pesos. The engineer José María Alexander made the plans in 1783 on behalf of the president of the court. Including Father Chamorro's expenses, it cost the municipality of Managua, a village at the time, 10,771.00 silver pesos. At that time Managua was reduced to this canton and its inhabitants chose this place because of its proximity to Lake Xolotlán, which provided them with food by catching sardines and other fish. The church of the priest Chamorro was completed in 1783.

In 1912, Saint Pope Pius X had created the Archdiocese of Managua, the Dioceses of León and Granada and the Apostolic Vicariate of Bluefields, since until then the only episcopal see was León.

Monsignor José Antonio Lezcano y Ortega was appointed Archbishop of Managua and the parish of Managua, located on the same site as the current building, was elevated to the category of Metropolitan Cathedral. Monsignor Lezcano, like the Prophet Haggai, insisted on the construction of a new building, which is why the old temple was demolished in 1925.

The first stone was laid on 5 April 1925 in a simple ceremony by Monsignor Lezcano and the President of Nicaragua, Carlos José Solórzano; however, the first design of the cathedral was published on 10 January 1926 and did not satisfy the Archbishop as it consisted of a large central nave and a separate bell tower opposite the temple. Monsignor Lezcano liked the photo of a church in Belgium and asked the engineer Pablo Dambach, of Swiss origin, to draw up the plans for the cathedral based on the photo of the Belgian church; the iron framework was brought from Belgium to Nicaragua by ship and transported by rail to Managua at the port of Corinto, Chinandega Department. Construction work on the Old Cathedral began in 1928. It was the first structure of this size to be built in reinforced concrete in the country. Three years after construction began on 31 March 1931, Holy Tuesday, an earthquake measuring 6.0 degrees on the Richter scale destroyed the capital, but not its metal frame, which withstood the quake. The building has Victorian designs of architecture with European, Renaissance and neoclassical replicas. >> [5]

If I take the centre of the church ruins (built from 1925), I reach the centre of the lagoon at 1865 metres, the south end at 2073 metres and the north side at 1657 metres.
(2073 + 1657) / 2 = 3730 / 2 = 1865 metres.

Tiscapa: Water supply since 25. Nov. 1888

The pond in Managua as a starting point still has the following information ready: Tiscapa means "mirror" in

---

[5]
https://es.wikipedia.org/wiki/Catedral_metropolitana_de_Santiago _apostol_de_Managua

Nahuat. José Santos Zelaya had a fort built on the Loma in 1894. On **25 November 1888**, a water supply was opened via pipes and pumps, with the flanks of the Loma forming the high point. [6] Who supported the construction? Germany?

Summary Distances

Starting point: Middle pond Laguna de Tiscapa	
Distance	**Object**
6 km	Laguna de Nejapa
60 km	Pacific coast to the south
600 km	Lago de Atilan (Guatemala)
6000 km	Great Slave Lake (Canada)
6000 km	Chain of Lakes (Argentina)

Besides:

Chain of Lakes (Argentina) (from WSW to ENE)	
Name	*Translation*
Laguna Epecuén	*Eternal spring*
Laguna del Venado	*Stag*
Laguna del Monte	*Mountain*
Laguna Cochico	*Piggy*
Laguna Alsina	*"family name"*
Laguna Inchauspe	*"family name"*

---

[6] https://de.wikipedia.org/wiki/Loma_de_Tiscapa#cite_ref-goni_5-0 (alcaldia managua Loma de Tiscapa)

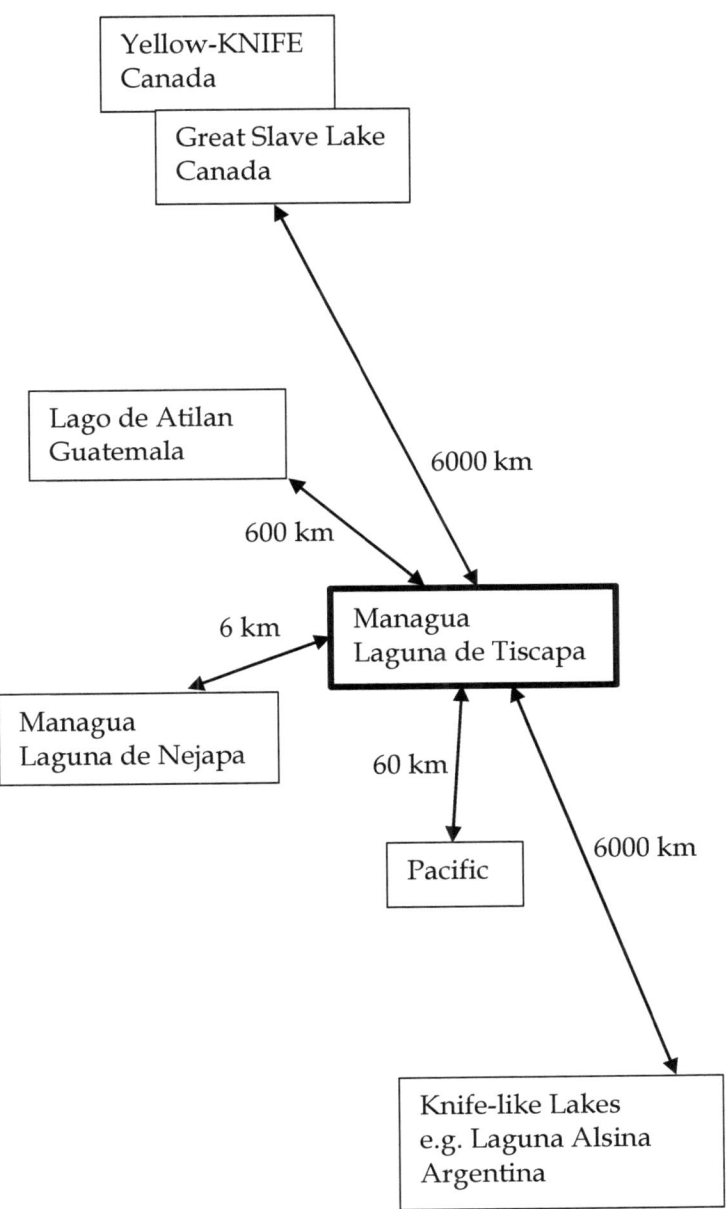

Yellow-KNIFE
Canada

Great Slave Lake
Canada

Lago de Atilan
Guatemala

6000 km

600 km

6 km

Managua
Laguna de Tiscapa

Managua
Laguna de Nejapa

60 km

Pacific

6000 km

Knife-like Lakes
e.g. Laguna Alsina
Argentina

Germans in Nicaragua since 1844

What could the Germans have to do with the six murders in Managua in 1889?
Relations with no other Central American state were as strong as with Nicaragua through the German Reich, and even before that through the Kingdom of Prussia. One could almost say it existed almost exclusively with this state in the 19th century. (At least that's how it seems to me).
I mention this because I assume that Jack the Ripper was a German, and he probably also did his mischief in Managua.

Bluefields (Nicaragua) at the atlantic coast

In 1844, Prince Carl of Prussia and Prince Otto Victor I of Schönburg-Waldenburg commissioned three emissaries to investigate whether the area around Bluefields was suitable for the establishment of a colony. In 1846, 107 colonists from Königsberg arrived in Bluefields, but their attempt to settle in Carlstadt, named after Prince Carl, son of Prince Otto Victor, failed: most of the settlers succumbed to tropical diseases; the survivors moved on to other colonies. Prince Otto Victor I of Schönburg-Waldenburg then persuaded the Moravian Church to start a mission there. In 1849 Heinrich Pfeiffer and Johann Lundberg, the first two missionaries, arrived. The Moravian Brethren, as they were called in Bluefield, shaped the religious, cultural and, in parts, the economic development of the village until well into the early 20th century. [7]

---

[7] https://de.wikipedia.org/wiki/Bluefields_(Nicaragua)

People Miskito, Religion German Community

The Miskito are an indigenous people who today live mainly on the Atlantic coast in the border region of Nicaragua and Honduras. Today, a good 100,000 people of this ethnic group live in Nicaragua.

The main settlement areas are in the Región Autónoma de la Costa Caribe Norte (Northern Atlantic Coast of Nicaragua, also called the Miskito Coast), with its capital Bilwi (Puerto Cabezas) and with the town Waspán on the river Wangki (Río Coco).

About 25,000 Miskitos live in Honduras today.

The name Miskito probably derives from the name of a former king, who was called Miskut. The Miskitos speak their own language - Miskito, for which a written language also exists. Many Miskito belong to the Moravian Church, i.e. the Moravian Church of the Herrnhut Brethren. [8]

Eisenstuck- Affair 1876–1878

The Eisenstuck Affair of 1876-1878 was a diplomatic-military dispute between the German Empire and the Republic of Nicaragua. In the process, the young Kaiserliche Marine, which was still in the process of being established, had one of its largest overseas military engagements to date. It took place on both the Pacific and Atlantic coasts.

The intervention was prompted by two raids on the Imperial Honorary Consul Paul Eisenstuck in the city of León in western Nicaragua in 1876. Eisenstuck had already been living in Central America for some time and was married

---

[8] https://de.wikipedia.org/wiki/Miskito

there. His stepdaughter Franziska was in marital strife and had fled with her child from her husband, a dentist from Leon, to her parents in 1875/76. According to historian Gerhard Wiechmann, she was the casus belli. The husband had not wanted to accept his wife's leaving and had violently attacked the Eisenstuck family and their daughter twice in the open street. During the first attack on 23 October 1876, three pistol shots were fired by the son-in-law, but they missed. The second assault on 29 November 1876 was much more brutal and was carried out by police soldiers who beat up and arrested the consul. Although Eisenstuck and his family were released on the way to court because of his diplomatic status, all criminal investigations against the perpetrators came to nothing. The criminal court referred to the path of a private prosecution and gave the incident the rank of a "family feud" in which the son-in-law was merely trying to win back his wife.

Germany saw international law damaged by the consul's disregard for immunity and refusal to take action against the perpetrators of the attacks. Germany demanded that Nicaragua punish the perpetrators, pay US$30,000 in compensation and have Nicaraguan soldiers salute the flag. Nicaragua did not comply because the foreign minister considered the matter to be a family matter and in his opinion the husband of the stepdaughter had had the right to take his wife back. Moreover, there were only about 100 Germans in Nicaragua at the time, so trade with the German Reich was small.

Throughout the affair, the Foreign Office made sure that Germany behaved in accordance with the valid norms of international law. It had its legal position confirmed several times by Great Britain and the USA. In accordance with the diplomatic practices of the time, Germany intensified the pressure, but at the same time called in the United Kingdom and the USA as mediators. The mediation was unsuccessful, especially since the Nicaraguan government treated the US diplomat so brusquely that the USA broke off diplomatic relations with Nicaragua until the end of the affair.

The Foreign Office finally asked the Imperial Admiralty for assistance in August 1877. The Admiralty sent the corvettes SMS Leipzig and SMS Ariadne from Germany and the corvette SMS Elisabeth from Japan, which was on a round-the-world voyage, to the west coast of Panama, where the three ships united on 9 March 1878 to form a squadron under Captain Wilhelm von Wickede and sailed to Corinto. Another ship, the cadet training ship SMS Medusa, was on a routine voyage in the West Indies and was ordered to the east coast of Nicaragua. The ships reached their destination on 17 and 18 March 1878. However, the ships were not equipped for landing operations and were therefore hardly in a position to exert military pressure on the government in the inland capital Managua.
There is a drawing with the following title:
"Salute of the Imperial War Flag by Nicaraguan Authorities, Corinto, Nicaragua, 31 March 1878. In the background, from left, SMS Ariadne, SMS Elisabeth and SMS Leipzig".

Nevertheless, the Nicaraguan government gave in on 31 March 1878. It paid compensation of US$ 30,000, the perpetrators were punished (fined US$ 500), and a detachment of marines rendered the flag salute. Not a shot was fired in the entire conflict.

The affair is an example of gunboat politics by European powers at the time. The young German Empire in particular was anxious to be taken seriously as a great power. This was related to national prestige aspirations, but also had a factual background. The treatment of foreign citizens abroad depended very much on the standing of their home country. The business of German merchants in Latin America therefore also depended on whether the governments there had respect for the German Reich.

Winning this respect for the Reich was one of the main tasks of the Kaiserliche Marine's foreign cruisers. It became apparent during the Eisenstuck affair that it was not capable of carrying out a landing operation against a Latin American state due to inadequate equipment. The fact that the operation nevertheless achieved the desired success can be attributed on the one hand to the diplomatic skills of the leader of the association, Wilhelm von Wickede, who was very experienced in Central America, and on the other hand to the fact that the German demand on Nicaragua was perceived as very moderate.

The attitude of the Nicaraguan government was contradictory. There is speculation among historians that the government hoped the Germans would shell opposition León, but this did not happen. For long-term German-Nicaraguan relations, the intervention was a heavy burden, nor was it supported by the small German colony of Nicaragua. It was not until 1896 that a trade treaty was concluded which, according to Houwald, "could make people forget" what had happened at the time. For the Nicaraguan politician and newspaper publisher Don Enrique Guzman, the day the $30,000 compensation was paid to the German Empire was a day of "national shame". [9]

---

[9] https://de.wikipedia.org/wiki/Eisenstuck-Affäre

Wilhelm von Wickede and Albrecht von Stosch

The name Albrecht von Stosch (living in Mittelheim, Rheingau) already appeared in my last book. Therefore, perhaps it is also quite interesting here.

On 17 September 1881 Wickede was promoted to Rear Admiral and in 1885 to Vice Admiral. He was Chief of Naval Station of the Baltic Sea from 1883 to 1887 and worked out an extended draft for naval tactics under Chief of Admiralty Albrecht von Stosch.

For five years, Wickede led the annual large squadron exercises and naval manoeuvres of the German fleet, but in 1887 he took a leave of absence due to illness. The real reason for his retirement, however, were disputes with Admiral von Stosch and his successor Caprivi about the training and deployment of warships in the merchant war. Wickede refused to let military-formal training be at the expense of professional parts. Together with the chief of the North Sea naval station, Vice-Admiral Count Monts, he also rejected merchant warfare as piracy vis-à-vis Caprivi. Wilhelm von Wickede died in Berlin on 28 November 1895. [10]

---

[10] https://de.wikipedia.org/wiki/Wilhelm_von_Wickede

Herrnhuter Brüdergemeine

The Moravian Church is a nominally interdenominational Christian faith movement that originated in the Bohemian Reformation (Bohemian Brethren) and was influenced primarily by Pietism, but also by Calvinism and (after the death of Zinzendorf in 1760) strongly by Lutheran Protestantism.
The largest Brethren congregation is currently in Tanzania.

Country, year of foundation, congregations, members
Caribbean & Latin America:

Costa Rica	1980/1941	3	1.900
Guyana	1878/1835	8	960
Honduras	1930	85	34.450
Jamaica	1754	65	8.100
Nicaragua	**1849**	**226**	**97.000**
Suriname	1735	67	30.000
West Indies -East	1732	52	15.100
Honduras (Mission Province of Nicaragua)			16.870
Cuba	1997		600

Here you can clearly see the focus on Nicaragua. The number of members is the highest in Latin America. In terms of the 3 states in Central America, the foundation is the oldest. [11]

---

[11] https://de.wikipedia.org/wiki/Herrnhuter_Brüdergemeine

Carl von Preußen

Prince Frederick Carl Alexander of Prussia (* 29 June 1801 at Charlottenburg Palace near Berlin; † 21 January 1883 in Berlin) was the third son of King Frederick William III and Queen Luise. He was a Prussian general.
Carl was described as "the most beautiful [of her] children" by his mother, who had already given birth to his siblings Friedrich Wilhelm (1795-1861), Wilhelm (1798-1888 as Emperor) and Charlotte (1798-1860 as Tsarina Alexandra Fyodorovna). After Carl, the siblings Alexandrine (1803-1892), Luise (1808-1870) and Albrecht (1809-1872) were born. Carl served as Governor of Mainz from 1864 to 1866. [12]

Otto Victor I. von Schönburg-Waldenburg

Otto Victor I von Schönburg-Waldenburg (* 1 March 1785 in Waldenburg (Saxony); † 16 February 1859 in Leipzig) was a member of the Saxon Parliament and Prince of Schönburg from 1800. [13]

Saxon Relationship with Hesse

In my opinion, the following are interesting
a) the relations to the Hessian princely houses [14] as well as to Sayn(-Wittgenstein-Berleburg), [15]

---

[12] https://de.wikipedia.org/wiki/Carl_von_Preußen
[13] https://de.wikipedia.org/wiki/Otto_Victor_I._von_Schönburg
[14] https://de.wikipedia.org/wiki/Hugo_zu_Schönburg-Waldenburg
[15] https://de.wikipedia.org/wiki/Otto_Friedrich_von_Schönburg-Waldenburg

b) that the first two sons of his eldest son Otto Friedrich (1819-1893) died very young in 1888.

Early death grandchildren 1888

Otto Friedrich's marriage to Pamela, née Freiin Łabuńska (* 31 August 1837; † 18 July 1901) produced seven children, including the two eldest sons:

Otto Carl Victor (* 1 May 1856; † 18 November 1888).
Lucie Princess of Sayn-Wittgenstein-Berleburg (1859-1903),

Otto Ludwig (* 29 March 1860; † 13 March 1888).

A son of Otto Carl Victor, Alexander, also dies at the age of 5 on 1 November 1888.

Reasons for murders in Managua?

Here are some speculations:

- Because of code "company, place, goods" the principals want to refer to the Spanish version of "Carl" (and thus indirectly also to the English one)
- German differences with the Nicaraguan government
- Disappointed about the failed succession to the Spanish throne 1868-1870 (too long ago, and actually has nothing to do with Central America)

Carlos and Charles Feigenbaum

Use spanish form of „Carl"

But perhaps it is more the case that for another code in this whole story, the hint is to use the Spanish form "Carlos" of "Carl".

Use english form of „Carl"

However, I also found out that the English form of "Carl", namely "Charles", must also be used to break another code. (See more below)

Family „Spanier"

Nowadays there is the "Spanier" winery in Gau-Bickelheim on the main road towards Wallertheim, i.e. near the cemetery. In the 1906 address book, however, there is no "Spanier" family in Gau-Bickelheim.
At that time, it only existed in Rhine-Hessian villages around Worms ... and also in Darmstadt.

But that has nothing to say in our context. Does it occur to you, because of London and Managua, that the German Empire sometimes sees English and Spanish as competitors? So there is no need to create a Carlos Feigenbaum out of a Spanish family.

Code „Carl Feigenbaum"

First bid from my side

I hereby make a first suggestion for a photo. If someone has a photo of a man who looks more like the drawing of Carl Feigenbaum, I would like it to come out. At the same time I combine the photo with an attempt to decipher a possible code in the alias name. But as it goes, someone else may come up with a different decryption.

Employee with company in Rheinhessen?

I received a copy of the picture from 1892 showing the employees of a company in Gau-Algesheim on the Rhine (between Bingen/Koblenz and Mainz) in 2000. The reason for this was my assumption that the oldest employee could be my great-great-grandfather Heinrich Hattemer VIII. (1830-1900), because he is registered in the church register as "worker at Avenarius" at the birth of his daughter Otilia in 1874. The second possibility: it is some other man from or around Gau-Algesheim. However, the older person, whom I would estimate to be between 55 and 60 years old, looks something like Carl Feigenbaum in the drawing before his execution in 1896.

Let's see how big the difference in appearance can be with
a) Photo from the front with hat, from the side without hat,
b) facial expressions before the arrest and after the conviction.

We also try to estimate the height.

If it really was Anton Zahn, then the company certainly had no idea that one of its employees might be working for the military intelligence service or high-ranking aristocrats of the German Reich.

Carlos Feigenbaum / Carbolineum

From Carlos Feigenbaum I can form the following word:
Carbolineum (11 Letters)
Carlos Fe**igenb**a**um** (5 of 6 + 6 of 10 Letters)
There remains: S, F, E, G, A (5 of 16 Letters)

Charles Feigenbaum / Gau-Algesheim

From Charles Feigenbaum I can form the following word:
Gau-Algesheim (12 Letters)
Char**les** F**eig**en**b**a**um** (5 of 7 + 7 of 10 Letters)
There remains: R, E, F, N, B (5 of 17 Letters)
Blemish: Insofar as I use a "C" for a "G.

Charles or Carlos Feigenbaum / Avenarius

Avenarius (9 Letters)
C**ar**los **Feige**nb**au**m (3 von 6 + 6 of 10 Letters)
There remains: C, L, O, G, E, B, M (7 of 16 Letters)
Ch**ar**les **Feige**n**bau**m (3 of 7 + 6 of 10 Letters)
There remains: C, H, L, E, G, E, B, M (8 of 17 Letters)
Blemish: The "V" is formed from the "F".

Here, the Spanish version is still more preferable, because it then means 3 out of **6 and 6** out of 10.

Nasty joke on company Avenarius?

The possible code would undoubtedly be a bad joke that someone is playing on the Avenarius company in Gau-Algesheim, which patented the product carbolineum as "Avenarius Carbolineum" in 1888 and was already selling it worldwide at the end of the 19th century.

Anton Zahn disguised as a merchant seaman?

If Anton Zahn alias Carl Feigenbaum (1841-1896) was a merchant seaman, i.e. transported goods across the seas, then he, if he was an employee, carried out the transport WITH the knowledge of the Avenarius company, for example several times to London in autumn 1888 and to Managua in January 1889.

Obviously, the port of departure, at least for London, was Bremerhaven. For according to Trevor Marriott, all crew lists from 1888 in Bremen have disappeared. And the ships "Reiher" and "Sperber" were registered in London as coming from Bremen. Only these ships come into question according to Marriott.

BUT: The killer contracts on the prostitutes in London and Managua were carried out WITHOUT the knowledge of the Avenarius company. One should assume this.

All statements are always made under the assumption that Anton Zahn was an employee of the Avenarius company in the first place.

Anton Zahn from Germany to the USA

In the photo in Gau-Algesheim from 1892 on the occasion of the 25th anniversary, there is a middle-level boss who was responsible for the USA business or overseas business, according to the testimony of Mr. Arnold Avenarius-Herborn.

The connections in the USA are strong. The head office there is in Milwaukee, Wisconsin. There are branches in New York, Seattle, New Orleans, etc.

The question is whether Anton Zahn, if he was an employee of the company at all, was still employed by Avenarius and working for the company in New York in August 1894 when he was arrested by the New York police.

Or had he already been dismissed; or did he resign himself? Really very striking is his property in Cincinnati.

Remaining letters

Can I still do something with the leftovers?

Out of Carlos Feigenbaum:
SFEGA
CLOGEBM
GAEMSGELB, CEMBALOS, FOLGSAME, GEFOLGES, LOBESAME, ABFOLGE, ABLOESE, ABSEGEL, BEFOLGE, GASOELE, OELGASE, GEFASEL, GEFOLGE, ABLEGE

Out of Charles Feigenbaum:
REFNB
CHLEGEBM
BREMEN   Rest: FCHLEGB, from this: BLECH (FG), CHEF, ELCH, FEHL, FLEH, GELB etc.
BLECHERNEM, FEHLMENGE, GEBRECHEN, BEFEHLEN, BELEHREN, BEGEHREN, BEHELFEN, ERGEBNEM, ERLEGNEM, **HERLEGEN,** HERGEBEN, BERECHNE, ERBLEHEN, BECHERN, BEFEHLE, BEGEBEN, BEGEHEN, BEHEBEN, BELEBEN, BELEHRE

Summary in tabular form

Carbolineum (11 Letters)

<u>Carlo</u>s Fe<u>igenba</u>um (5 of 6 + 6 of 10 Letters)

Alias	Alias No.	Goods	Alias No.
C	1	C	1
A	2	A	2
R	3	R	3
L	4	B	13
<u>O</u>	<u>5</u>	<u>O</u>	<u>5</u>
<u>S</u>	<u>6</u>	L	4
		I	9
F	7	N	12
E	8	E	8
I	9	U	15
G	10	M	16
E	11		
N	12		
B	13		
A	14		
U	15		
M	16		

Gau-Algesheim (12 Letters)

<u>Cha</u>r<u>l</u>es F<u>eig</u>en<u>baum</u> (5 of 7 + 7 of 10 Letters)

Alias	Alias No.	Place	Alias No.
C	1	G	1 (*)
<u>H</u>	**<u>2</u>**	A	3
A	3	U	16
R	4	-	
L	5	A	15
<u>E</u>	*<u>6</u>*	L	5
<u>S</u>	**<u>7</u>**	G	11
		E	9
F	8	**<u>S</u>**	**<u>7</u>**
E	9	**<u>H</u>**	**<u>2</u>**
I	10	E	12
G	11	I	10
E	12	M	17
N	13		
B	14		
A	15		
U	16		
M	17		

(*) C treats as G

Avenarius (9 Letters)

Carlos Feigenbaum (3 of 6 + 6 of 10 Letters)

Alias	Alias No.	Chef	Alias No.
C	1	A	2
A	2	V	7 (**)
R	3	E	8
L	4	N	12
O	*5*	A	14
S	**6**	R	3
		I	9
F	7	U	15
E	8	**S**	**6**
I	9		
G	10		
E	11		
N	12		
B	13		
A	14		
U	15		
M	16		

(**) F treats as V

Avenarius (9 Letters)

Ch**arles** **Fei**ge**n**b**au**m (3 of 7 + 6 of 10 Letters)

Alias	Alias No.	Chef	Alias No.
C	1	A	3
_H_	_2_	V	8 (**)
A	3	E	9
R	4	N	13
L	5	A	15
_E_	_6_	R	4
_S_	_7_	I	10
		U	16
F	8	_S_	_7_
E	9		
I	10		
G	11		
E	12		
N	13		
B	14		
A	15		
U	16		
M	17		

(**) F treats as V

Do we have any coding at all? If so, is the code to be looked for in exactly the three parameters: place, name, goods? Again, I am open to other suggestions. Certainly, the matter is poorly researched and requires comparison with huge databases. That is why I ask that other people take another look at the matter.

Search for alternative companies

In Gau-Algesheim, the company of Georg Presser (1835-1898) also distributed carbolineum since 1862. [16] Two elements (carbolineum and Gau-Algesheim) are the same when matched with Carl/Carlos/Charles Feigenbaum. The company name Presser cannot fit because of the double S and the double R alone. This website in the footnote lists 20 companies that already existed in Rheinhessen in 1888: [17] Please ask experts to look for further possibilities here.

Search for alternative locations

Should I look for other companies in other places with other products? How about Gau-Bickelheim instead of Gau-Algesheim? There I have no second "i" in Charles Feigenbaum and no "k" at all.
More places would have to be investigated.
If one is convinced that the murderer comes from the area around Bingen and Alzey, only places there need to be investigated. "Geisenheim" (other side of the Rhine) has the letters, but one "i" too many.

Search for alternative goods

The easiest way is to try to make another word out of carbolineum. The result is something like "Carbolin" (carboline) or "Uranblei" (uranium lead), "Leinbaum" (linseed tree), albumen, etc. [18] Which company fits?

---

[16] https://www.brilmayer-gesellschaft.de/annoncen-aus-zeitungen-und-festbuechern/carbolineum.html
[17] https://www.wirtschaftsgeschichte-rlp.de/aufsaetze/unternehmen-aus-rheinhessen.html
[18] https://www.wort-suchen.de/buchstabensalat-loesen/

Another photo of Jacob Köth III.

*My great-grandparents Heinrich Diegel and Helena Wetzel on
their wedding day in Sprendlinger Str. 36 on 25 July 1903.
Behind them: left Jakob Köth III and on the right Philipp Maus.*

I have obtained the birth entry of Jacob Köth III from the Protestant parish office on 1 April 1850. Parents: Johann Köth I. and Anna Marg. née Geier. (Geier = vulture)

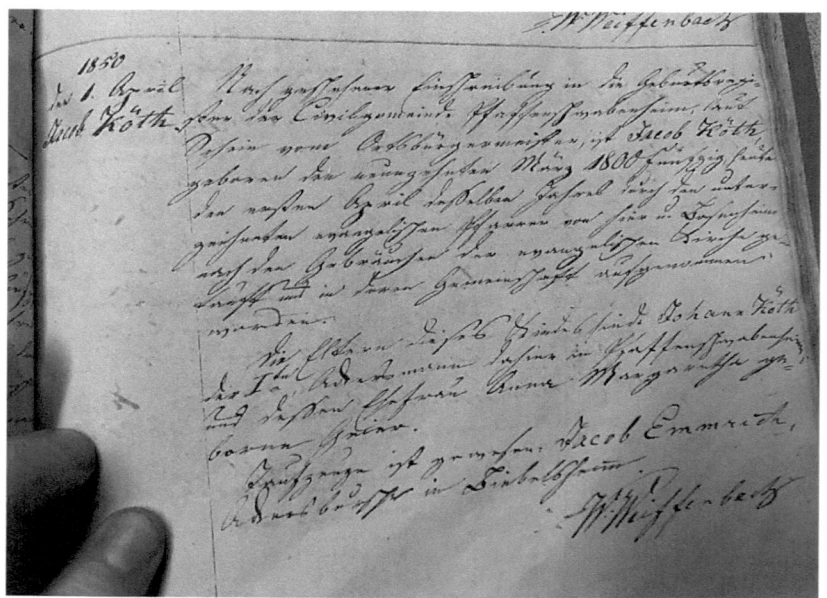

On Jacob Köth, see my two books on Jack the Ripper from 2015 and 2021 (photo there as on page 79).

Birth of Maria Elisabetha Barth née Köth, died in Lonsheim (end of the 1+8+8+8 km from Bingen) on 12 March 1824 in Pfaffen-Schwabenheim.

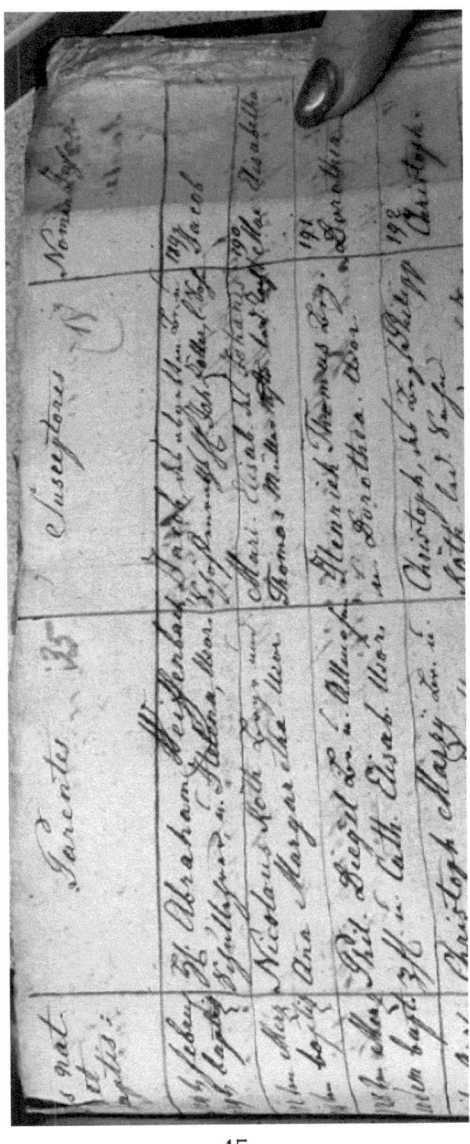

Data Carl Feigenbaum 1894: 163.6 cm

The following data were recorded about him after his arrest in August 1894 from Sing Sing Prison near New York.:

This is the only known description of Carl Feigenbaum:

Born – Germany
Age – 54
Married [It is unclear whether the prison officer dealing with the form wrote this on it expecting 'yes' or 'no' in response, or whether Feigenbaum himself indicated that he was married.]
Occupation – Florist
Height – 5.4ins
Weight – 126lbs
Religion – Catholic
Complexion – medium

Read – Yes
Write – Yes
Smoke – Yes
Shoe size – 8
Hat size – 6–7
Hair – Dark Brown thin on top of head
Eyes – Grey, Small deep set
Forehead – High and heavily arched
Nose – Large, Red with pimples
Teeth – Poor nearly all gone on left side
Tattoos – Anchor in Indian ink on right hand at base of thumb
Habits – MAD!

That is a good description. [19]
To what extent the height is rounded up or down is unclear.
5 feet 4 inches may be 5 feet 4.4 inches (163.6 cm).

Age is given as 54 when he was admitted to prison in August 1894. I had found Anton Zahn's birth entry on 17 May 1841 in the Gau-Bickelheim Catholic church register.
In Wikipedia, the year of birth is given as 1840, and the place of birth as Karlsruhe. But that is where the noble client comes from, not Carl Feigenbaum. That's just what he's supposed to say to the US authorities.
Everything is covered in detail in a previous book of mine.

What else comes to my mind about the age would be:
Carl Feigenbaum alias Anton Zahn probably means "in his 54th year", so he would then be 53 years old in August 1894.
Then the birth on 17 May 1841 would be correct.

Why does he say he is a "florist"? In German, that's probably a "Blumenhändler".
Blumen, bitumen, coal tar?
Bitumen is not in carbolineum, but the material refers to a similar industry.

---

[19] Marriott, Trevor: Jack the Ripper, The 21th Century Investigation

47

Group picture 1892 – Anton Zahn?

Appearance of the man, „Shabby-genteel"

Elegant shirt collar, but shabby cardigan patched at the right armpit. Jack the Ripper was: "genteel- shabbily dressed". Appearance similar to Carl Feigenbaum.

Knife, Left-handed

In the group picture you can see from the direction of the writing on the 3 barrels in the foreground and on the knife that the person was left-handed, just like Jack the Ripper.

Estimation of body size plank to hat

As can be seen from the group photo, the back row of men is standing on planks/boards which were presumably (not visible) placed on upright wooden barrels. At the right edge, the plank overhangs a little, so that despite being covered by the front row of people, it is visible at what height above the ground the bodies of the back row below end.

The picture was taken in the German Reich (not in the USA) with a middle-level boss who was responsible for business in the USA. Mr. Arnold Avenarius-Herborn confirmed this to me. But he also wrote that the brick wall behind the people has not existed like that for 70 years, in Gau-Algesheim. This is because the courtyard has been built over since then. Besides, the wall is plastered. So you can't measure what the height of the bricks is, as a comparative size or reference for height.

A standard measurement in the German Empire from 1870/71 onwards was 65 mm height of the bricks and clinkers and 10 mm mortar. Older houses in Rheinhessen, for example, have a height of 70 mm. [20]

The barrel diameters at the head end are also unknown.
So all that remains is the average eye distance of the men looking directly into the camera. About 7 people do this. I set the average at 65 mm. Because the interpupillary distance is 65 mm on average (even for smaller people), I can determine with a certain tolerance that the bricks actually have a height of 65 mm. [21]

---

[20] http://www.fotografie-architektur.de/stockphoto-galerie-5-z06.html
[21] https://de.wikipedia.org/wiki/Augenabstand

The three barrels in the photo then have a diameter of 60 cm and could even be 300 litre barrels.

22 ½ Bricks with 22 layers of mortar: 165.3 cm

The probably oldest man, who looks something like Carl Feigenbaum (or am I mistaken), covers 22 ½ bricks with 22 layers of mortar with his body.

That makes a distance of:
(65mm times 22.5) + (10mm times 22) = 1462.5 + 220
= 1682.5 mm

I have to subtract the heel of the shoe. It can be between 1.5 to 3 cm. Maximum subtraction of 30 mm gives:
1682.5 mm - 30 mm = **165.25 cm** (-1-)

The oldest man would thus be 3 cm too tall compared to the record of Sing Sing Prison near New York, where Carl Feigenbaum is 5 feet and 4 inches, that is 162.65 cm tall.

All the men are wearing hats. There is some uncertainty in that. How far does the head run into the hat?
To do this, look at the distance from the chin to the mouth and from the mouth to the eyes. From this, the height of the forehead can be approximately determined.

Body height = 7 to 7.5 times head height: 163.8 cm

There is also the rule that the height of the body is 7 to 7.5 times the height of the head of a man. [22]

---

[22] https://de.wikipedia.org/wiki/Körperproportion OR
https://en.wikipedia.org/wiki/Body_proportions

Here, too, there is uncertainty in the hat area. If we look at the photo, we can estimate the head to be
(65mm times 3) + (10mm times 3) = 226 mm (head height)
This limits the body height between:
Lower limit: 226 times 7 = 1582 mm
Upper limit: 226 times 7.5 = 1695 mm

The first value is far below the 5 feet 4 inches and the second value is far above.
The average is 226 times 7.25 = **163.85 cm** (-2-)

The average factor of 7.25 results in a height that is too high by 1638.5 minus 1626.5 = 12 mm, i.e. 1.2 cm too high. Rounding tolerance?

5 feet 4 inch should mean maximum: 5 feet 4.4 inch.
5 times 30.48 + 4.4 ti. 2.54 = 152.4 + 11.176 = **163.58 cm**. (-3-)

Spelling mistake in Sing Sing, New York? - No!

Is there a spelling mistake in Sing Sing prison? It happens that people confuse the number 4 with 7 because these (besides 1) do not have roundings like the other digits. I once confused "S" and "2" when writing on the blackboard in chemistry class.

With 5 feet and 7 inches, Carl Feigenbaum would be 170.18 cm tall.
5 times 30.48 + 7 times 2.54 = 152.4 + 17.78 = 170.18 cm
This would be too tall compared to the 1892 photo.

How does his body weight fit with his official height of 5 feet 4 inches = 162.56 cm?
(5 times 30.48 + 4 times 2.54 = 152.4 + 10.16 = 162.56 cm)

There are 126 lbs.
126 times 0.453592 = 57.15 kg
At 5 feet 4 inches it is normal weight.
At 5 feet 7 inches it is ideal weight.

Does Carl Feigenbaum look emaciated and gaunt in the drawing in prison or at his sentencing in 1896?
Hence only 57 kg?
Does the drawing say anything when Feigenbaum was in the electric chair in 1896? Standard dimensions of electric chairs, bent legs (knees) or free-floating feet.
The man to the right of the oldest person is taller. The other men in the upper, back row are mostly or all boys. Are they really all boys, at what age? Are they still growing?

Average size births 1840 in Europe: 163.8 cm

What is the average height in Rheinhessen at that time, which should rather be compared to France or even Italy because of their ancestors from the times since the Roman Empire?

The average for people born around 1840 in

France 164.3 cm
Italy 162 cm
Germany 166.6 cm (1850: only 163.8 cm) [23]

Carl Feigenbaum is therefore pretty much on the average for height at the time.

---

[23] https://de.statista.com/statistik/daten/studie/472464/umfrage/
historische-entwicklung-der-menschlichen-koerpergroesse-in-
ausgewaehlten-laendern/

The information in Sing Sing prison is probably correct after comparison with weight and comparison with the average in Europe at that time.

Length of the Knife: 20 cm

A: Gau-Algesheim 1892

The knife on the company picture from Gau-Algesheim from 1892 has a length like
- 4 layers of bricks of 65 mm each
- 5 layers of mortar of 10 mm each
The dimensions are
4 times 65 mm + 5 times 10 mm = 260 mm +50 mm = 310 mm (Without the handle, which is 10 to 12 cm long, it is approx. 20 cm).

B: London 1888

Nichols: These cuts had also been inflicted with the same knife, estimated to be at least 6–8 inches (15–20 cm) long, and possibly a cork-cutter or shoemaker's knife. [24]

Chapman: Very sharp knife with a thin narrow blade and must have been at least 6 to 8 inches in length, probably longer. [25]

The mutilations to Eddowes's body had all been inflicted with a knife at least six inches in length after death. [26]

---

[24] https://en.wikipedia.org/wiki/Mary_Ann_Nichols
[25] https://en.wikipedia.org/wiki/Annie_Chapman
[26] https://en.wikipedia.org/wiki/Catherine_Eddowes

C: Comparison London with Gau-Algesheim

According to reports by the medical experts who examined the victims in London in 1888, the knife was about 20 cm long in Nichols', Chapman's and Eddowes' case.

In the 1892 photo in Gau-Algesheim, according to estimates against other objects, it is about 30 cm long, but with a handle.

If you subtract 10 cm / 12 cm handle, you get 20 cm / 18 cm free blade length.

In addition, there is talk of a rounded tip on Jack the Ripper, which can be found in the 1892 photo.

D: More information about 1892 Photo

A slightly rounded tip is followed by a triangle that transitions into a long rectangle. Under the man's cardigan is the transition from the free blade to the handle.

The rectangle has a width of (65+10)/2 mm = 3.75 cm.

The height of the triangle is about the same: 3.75 cm.

The knife is pushed into the cardigan with protective tape.

On the following page:
- Barrel 1: Original Carbolineum Avenarius Patent ... 1867
- Barrel 2: C W 25 Milwaukee ...
- Barrel 3: New Orleans 1892
- On the far right the man is holding a board with "Milwaukee".
- On the circular stencil of the jack: "Osiris".

All this makes no statement as to whether the company indirectly and without its knowledge via "mole" Anton Zahn (employee?) has any relation to the Jack-the-Ripper actions.

Abuse of global corporate network

Carbolineum in Nicaragua

On 9 March 1897, there is the first definite reference to carbolineum in Nicaragua. At that time, the German consul Wiesicke noted: "The obligations regarding the import of carbolineum are falling away. Above all for killing insects, the substance is used in Nicaragua." [27]

Accordingly, there were already imports of carbolineum (probably also from Germany) some years before 1897.

CARBOLINEUM IN NICARAGUA.

On the 9th of March, 1897, the Government of Nicaragua issued a decree by which the duties on the importation of carbolineum are abolished.

Carbolineum, or crude carbolic acid, is used in this country to a great extent for the killing of insects, and will find a ready market here at this time of the year, when the dry season is giving place to the rainy one and obnoxious insects are abundant.

PAUL WIESIKE,

MANAGUA, *March 15, 1897.*   *Consul.*

Avenarius Carbolineum in Great Britain

There is an advertisement for "Carbolineum Avenarius" in the Welsh newspaper "Y Werin" of 7 January 1888, where "Peters, Bartsch, And Co., Derby" is mentioned. [28]

Peters, name from Northern Germany - Bartsch, name from the East (Silesia, Posen and Prussia). Derby is situated between Birmingham and Sheffield or Manchester.

---

[27] Consular Reports: Commerce, manufactures, etc, Ausgaben 200-203
[28] https://papuraunewydd.llyfrgell.cymru/view/3696628

Address of the London sales office was 116 Newgate Street. [29] (So unlike Aldgate, near Mitre Square).
There is a letter written in German from the company in Derby to a Saxon customer in Oberlungwitz (Written as "Aberlungwitz"). [30]

Avenarius Carbolineum in the USA

In the Handbook for the Preservation of Wood (Wood Preservation) of 1916, it is stated, among other things, that a company was established in New Orleans in 1888. There is no mention of the Avenarius company here. However, elsewhere the headquarters in Milwaukee is mentioned. [31]

1887. Southern Pacific Railway (Atlantic System) began treating Texas pine ties by the Burnett process at a leased plant.

1888. New Orleans Wood-Preserving Company erected a plant at New Orleans, La., to treat ties by the Burnett process, and piles and lumber by creosoting, for Texas & New Orleans Railroad.

1889. Southern Pacific Railway built a plant at West Oakland, Cal., employing either the Bethell or Curtis & Isaacs creosoting processes for treating ties and piles.

Avenarius Carbolineum. Carbolineum Wood Preserving Co., Milwaukee, Wis., New York.

Barol. Anthrol Wood Preserving Co., New York.

Barrett Grade One Liquid Creosote Oil (Carbosota). The Barrett Co., 17 Battery Place, New York; Birmingham, Ala.; Boston, Mass.; Chicago, Ill.; Cincinnati, O.; Cleveland, O.; Detroit, Mich.; Kansas City, Mo.; Louisville, Ky.; Minneapolis, Minn.; Nashville, Tenn.; New Orleans, La.; Peoria, Ill.; Philadelphia, Pa.; Pittsburgh, Pa.; St. Louis, Mo.; Salt Lake City, Utah; Seattle, Wash.

---

[29] https://www.andrewsgen.com; http://specialcollections.le.ac.uk
[30] https://picclick.de/DERBY-Brief-1902-Peters-Bartsch-Co-313043762147.html
[31] https://www.woodworkersuk.co.uk/books/handbook-on-wood-preservation-1916.pdf

The Columbus (Ohio) Railroad Company uses Avenarius Carbolineum in 1891. [32]

In a German-language newspaper from 1895 we also find an informative advertisement for the remedy: [33]

In the Seattle newspaper "Builder & Engineer" of 1907, Avenarius Carbolineum is presented very broadly. It refers to the branches in Portland, Denver and San Francisco. [34] (see on the internet)

---

[32] www.alamy.it Darin: Il gionale ferraviario di strada, Fig 5
[33] https://chroniclingamerica.loc.gov/
[34]
https://spl.contentdm.oclc.org/digital/collection/p16118coll26/id/1098/

Photo of Jack the Ripper?

Carl Feigenbaum laterally! - and also frontally?

CARL FEIGENBAUM.
Electrocuted at Sing Sing Yesterday for the Murder of Mrs. Hoffmann.

Prerequisite (was dealt with by me in 2015/2021):
Carl Feigenbaum = Anton Zahn (1841-96) = Jack the Ripper.
If Carl Feigenbaum, who is electrocuted in Sing Sing prison, is Jack the Ripper, the drawing on the left depicts the "monster" of London.

Question about the photo (detail) on the right:
Is the employee in the photo of the company Anton Zahn?

Search for clues:
- Comparison of face between drawing and photo,
- comparison of Jack the Ripper's style of dress with photo

- Comparison of the statement "left-handed" with photo
- Comparison of height on photo with Sing Sing note
- knife at all and type of knife, a sailor's cap

What speaks against it

Company Avenarius had opened a new sales office in Hamburg on 17.1.1891. This could be the reason why the employee is wearing a kind of "Prince Heinrich cap". [35]
Is the man in the 1892 photo too tall and of another age?
Left- or right-handed, position of beard.

Comparison JtR – C. Feigenbaum – Man on photo

Person / Property	Jack the Ripper	Carl Feigenbaum	Man on photo 1892
Body size	*5 feet 5 inch?*	5 feet 4 inch	5 feet 5 inch
Sailor	Tr. Marriott Assumption	Statement: been at sea	Prince Henry Cap
Appearance	*unclear*	Drawing	*Like drawing*
Clothes	Shabby-genteel	*unclear*	Shabby-genteel
Knife	YES	YES	YES
Left-handed	*Depends on the position*	*unclear*	YES

Israel Schwartz told investigators he had seen Stride being attacked outside Dutfield's Yard at approximately 12:45 a.m. by a man with dark hair, a small brown moustache and approximately 5 feet 5 inches in height. [36]

---

[35] https://www.zobodat.at/pdf/Ent-Mitt-Zool-Mus-Hamburg_4_0035-0048.pdf
[36] https://en.wikipedia.org/wiki/Elizabeth_Stride

Variations in appearance

Front and side view – Albert Fish

Albert Fish in the year 1903
Photos from the side without hat and from the front with hat. [37]

Albert Fish (* 19 May 1870 in Washington, D.C. as Hamilton Howard Fish; † 16 January 1936 in Sing Sing, Ossining) was a US serial killer and cannibal. [38]
You can see from him how strong the difference of the face (emotional impression) can be laterally/frontally.

---

[37]   http://www.nydailynews.com/new-york/1928-murder-grace-budd-albert-fish-gallery-1.1277430?pmSlide=10 (Wikipedia (ital.))
[38] Via Wikipedia (en.): Albert Fish. In: Academic Dictionaries and Encyclopedias. (en-academic.com [retrieved on 17. September 2021]).

It also fits perfectly with the comparison with Carl Feigenbaum alias Anton Zahn, because Albert Fish wears a hat in the front view and none in the side view. Because shortly before the execution, Carl Feigenbaum is drawn from the side and WITHOUT a hat. The person in the group picture in 1892 has the frontal view and WITH a hat.

Before arrest, after judgement – Johann Otto Hoch

Johann Otto Hoch before arrest and after death sentence [39]

In him one can see the difference in mental condition, a) in freedom without charges a few years before 1906 and presumably b) when the death sentence was pronounced. Here, too, the comparison with Carl Feigenbaum is almost ideal, because:
Self-confident J. Otto Hoch alias Johann Schmitt is taken frontally and "bent" from the side.

---

[39]   http://www.executedtoday.com/2012/02/23/1906-johann-otto-hoch-bluebeard/ (Wikipedia (engl.))
https://murderpedia.org/male.H/h/hoch-johann-photos.htm

Agent, not known by Avenarius

Anton Zahn – Leverages business relationships?

If Anton Zahn was an employee at the Avenarius company (and perhaps he is the oldest man in the 1892 photo), then he could have been recruited by someone outside the company for the Jack the Ripper operation.

His boss, Richard Avenarius (1840 - 1917), knew nothing of all this.

The abuse of the company could be proven if documents were found in which Anton Zahn alias Carl Feigenbaum was a merchant seaman on very specific ships that were in question at the time of the crimes in London and Managua, travelling on behalf of the company, officially to distribute carbolineum.

This company is certainly only one example. I would be glad if other people could clarify whether other companies also come into question and whether it had to go through a company as a cover at all. Perhaps there are other parameters than "place, company, goods" in which "Carl Feigenbaum" is coded. Only which ones?

A construction company from the same town, founded in 1887, has 2 "R" (the "Z" could come from the "S" if necessary), as does a company in neighbouring Ingelheim. However, the same letter does not have to be used twice in my example.

I have taken the life of the head of the company, who was not guilty of anything, from the Internet below:

Richard Avenarius (1840 – 1917): blameless

Richard Ernst Abundius Avenarius (* 9 April 1840 in Koblenz; † 1 February 1917 in Gau-Algesheim) was a German chemist and entrepreneur.

Richard Avenarius was born on 9 April 1840 in Koblenz into one of the city's leading families. His parents were Amalie née Maehler (1813-1892) and Albert Avenarius (1813-1871), who was civilian director of garrison administration in Koblenz and later in Mainz. His maternal grandfather was Abundius Maehler (1777-1853), who was Lord Mayor of Koblenz from 1818 to 1847.

Later, the family moved from the capital of the Prussian Rhine Province to the Grand Ducal Hessian Mainz, where he took his Abitur in 1860. He then did his military service, from which he retired after an accident, and then studied chemistry. In 1866 Richard Avenarius took part in the German War as a Landwehr officer in the Prussian Lower Rhine Fusilier Regiment No. 39 and in the Franco-Prussian War in 1870/71. He was awarded the Iron Cross and promoted to captain before retiring as an invalid in 1871.

As early as 1867, Richard Avenarius married his wife Angelika (née Maeckler, 1839-1910), to whom he was married until her death. Their only child Albert died in infancy in 1879. In 1894, the couple founded the Albertus Hospital in Gau-Algesheim in memory of their son, which still exists today in a modified form.

In 1869, Richard founded the company Gebr. Avenarius in Gau-Algesheim together with his brother Carl Avenarius. Initially, they operated an existing boiler forge there for the production of pressure cookers and steam wash boilers, among other things. Later they built a creosote factory for impregnating wood. In 1876, the company launched the wood preservative carbolineum, which became a great commercial success.

The Avenarius brothers founded branches in Berlin, Hamburg and Cologne, as well as further factories in Adlershof near Berlin, Amstetten in Lower Austria, Pressburg in Austria-Hungary and St Petersburg in Russia. A factory was also built in Milwaukee in the USA, with branches in the USA, Canada and Mexico.

In 1908, the company launched the liquid metal cleaning agent GAGA, named after the first letters of the company Gebr. Avenarius, Gau-Algesheim, which was also very successful.

Richard Avenarius was one of the leading men of the National Liberal Party in the Grand Duchy of Hesse. In 1902, he was awarded the honorary title of Kommerzienrat and the Cross of Honour of the Grand Ducal Hessian Order of Merit for his services.

In 1908, Avenarius took over the chairmanship of the Rheinhessen Bismarck Association and was thus instrumental in the construction of the Bismarck Tower on the Westerberg near Gau-Algesheim and Ingelheim am Rhein, which was inaugurated in 1912. As early as 1909, Richard Avenarius had a lookout point with a refuge built on the Westerberg near Gau-Algesheim, which has borne the name Richardshöhe since 1911.

In 1914, Richard Avenarius adopted his nephew Heinrich Herborn (1873-1955), a chemist with a doctorate, who had worked in the company since 1898 and had been a partner since 1911. In 1917, Heinrich Avenarius-Herborn became the sole owner of the company Gebr. Avenarius.

Richard Avenarius died on 1 February 1917 at the age of 76 in Gau-Algesheim and was buried there. [40]

The address book Rheinhessen of 1906 lists the home of Richard Avenarius at Ingelheimerstraße 11 in Gau-Algesheim. He is a factory owner, a retired captain, and a member of the district committee. And he is mentioned with his factory: Gebrüder Avenarius, Karbolineumfabrik und Imprägnier-Anstalt (Avenarius Brothers, Carbolineum Factory and Impregnating Institute).

He (as well as Koser, Schüller etc.) has no connection to the Jack-the-Ripper action.

Carbolineum 1888 as Brand

Carbolineum (from Latin carbo 'coal' and oleum 'oil') also carbolineum or coal tar oil is an oily, water-insoluble, flammable, brown-red, tarry-smelling, high-boiling distillate of coal tar.
Coal tar distillates were first used as wood preservatives in 1838 by Bethell in Great Britain. The name carbolineum was introduced as a trademark by the Avenarius company in 1888. It is originally made from filtered anthracene oil, which is distilled and filtered again. (Avenarius). However, anthracene oil that has only been filtered once is also called carbolineum. It is usually provided with further additives such as chlorine zinc, chlorine (Avenarius Carbolineum, German Imperial Patent (D.R.P.) 46021/1888), copper salts (Barol), phenol as well as resins in order to adjust the chemical properties. Etc. etc. [41]

---

[40] https://de.wikipedia.org/wiki/Richard_Ernst_Abundius_Avenarius
[41] https://de.wikipedia.org/wiki/Carbolineum

Coal Hole + Wood = Carbolineum?

The head of Catherine Eddowes was resting on „**coal hole**".
At 1:44 a.m., Eddowes's mutilated and disembowelled body
was found lying on her back, with her head resting on a coal
hole and turned towards the left shoulder, in the south-west
corner of Mitre Square by policeman Edward Watkins. [42]
Carbolineum comes from lat. carbo ‚Coal' and oleum ‚Oil'.
Coal; Hole = converted to Oehl (Öl). (german for Oil)
In Annie Chapman's case it is: Phillips also observed six
areas of blood spattering upon the wall of the house between
the steps and **wooden palings** dividing 27 and 29 Hanbury
Street. [43] Just as trees and wooden posts are impregnated
with carbolineum, wooden posts were brushed with blood.

Cuts from left to right

The injuries at Mary Ann Nichols were from left to right and
might have been done by a left-handed person. [44]
Chapman's throat had been cut from left to right so deeply
the bones of her vertebral column bore striations. [45]
Stride: she was killed by a single, swift slash wound from
left to right across her neck. [46]

---

[42] https://en.wikipedia.org/wiki/Catherine_Eddowes
[43] https://en.wikipedia.org/wiki/Annie_Chapman
[44] https://en.wikipedia.org/wiki/Mary_Ann_Nichols
[45] https://en.wikipedia.org/wiki/Annie_Chapman
[46] https://en.wikipedia.org/wiki/Elizabeth_Stride

Cover Name Feigenbaum on ship?

The following is very speculative:

Anton Zahn, perhaps an employee of the Avenarius company, is possibly commissioned by his boss in 1888 to arrange matters involving carbolineum in London (or Derby). Richard Avenarius believes Anton Zahn is only travelling on behalf of the company.

In truth, he is given the alias "Carl Feigenbaum" on the ship "Reiher", which starts in Bremerhaven and makes for London, from 1888 onwards, by the principals I tried to identify in my last book.

So it might be an option:

In London he does his business. And afterwards, at night and with the help of at least one German companion, he goes after the selected prostitutes.

Richard Avenarius in Gau-Algesheim on the Rhine knows nothing about the extra assignment from the German conspirators.

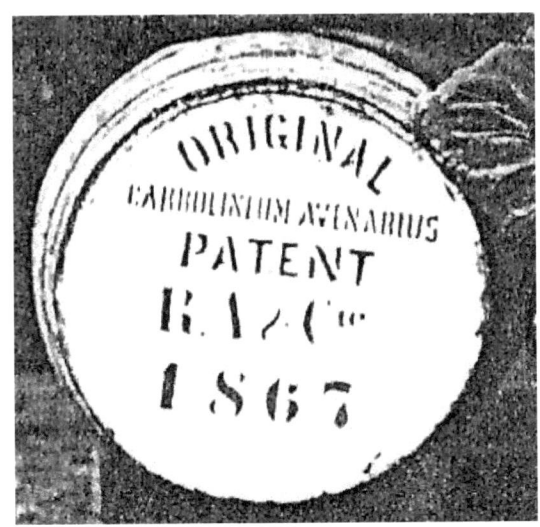

Avenarius' honourable ancestors

Grandfather Abundius Maehler, OB Koblenz

Abundius Maehler (* 1 June 1777 in Ehrenbreitstein; † 18 February 1853 in Niederheimbach) was Lord Mayor of Koblenz from 1818 to 1847. [47]

Maehler was the son of Franz Josef Maehler and Anna Johanna née Vacano. After studying in Giessen, he became a court clerk in Virneburg in 1798. From 1805 to 1814 Maehler was notary in Mayen. In October 1814 he became office administrator of the district administration Koblenz under Austro-Bavarian administration. After the Rhineland was taken over by Prussia, he took up a position as district police inspector in Koblenz. When the Prussian government was established, he became government secretary with the prospect of being promoted to government councillor. In this capacity he was also one of the directors of the Koblenz pawnshop from 2 June 1817.

On 26 March 1818, Maehler was appointed Lord Mayor and Police Director of Koblenz. His almost 30-year term of office was marked by diligence and loyalty. During this time, he personally recorded the minutes of every meeting of the city council. His willingness to help has also been handed down; he mediated in conflicts between citizens and the Prussian state. In 1819, he warned his schoolmate and supporter of the French Revolution, Joseph Görres, of his imminent arrest.

---

[47] https://de.wikipedia.org/wiki/Abundius_Maehler

Relationship with Crown Prince of Prussia

His term of office included the construction of the ship bridge over the Rhine (1819), the creation of the main cemetery (1820), the donation of the ruins of Stolzenfels Castle to Crown Prince Friedrich Wilhelm IV (1823), the founding of a public library (1827), the establishment of a chamber of commerce (1834) and the conclusion of a contract for the supply of gas to the city (1845).
There is a portrait of the man on the internet.

Father (+1871) in Koblenz and Mainz

Albert Avenarius (1813-1871) was civilian director of garrison administration in Koblenz and later in Mainz.

Cross-checking the 6s distances

In my previous book I had almost always calculated the Google Maps distances using the coordinates and additionally checked them in maps.
Here I limit the control to maps from the "Universal Atlas, Die Welt in Karten" by RV-Verlag.

P. 127: 60 km to Pacific, 600 km to Guatemala Lake Atitlan
P.130/131: 6000 km to chain of lakes in Argentina
p. 110/111: 6000 km to Great Slavic Lake in Canada

Measured with the ruler I get 58.5 km, 605 km, 5860 km to Yellowknife and 5830 km to Lakes Argentina.
The ruler is only accurate to 1 mm and the curvature of the earth plays a role. So it should fit with Google Maps.

Something from the film 1988

In the 1988 film with actor Michael Caine as Inspector Frederick Abberline, the murder of Annie Chapman shows the killer neatly laying out the victim's belongings. As if, in my opinion, he wanted to point out the meaningful geometry of the first four murders. Wikipedia says:
<< Jack the Ripper is a 1988 Anglo-American co-production by Thames Television and CBS television film drama based on the notorious Jack the Ripper murder spree in Victorian London. It was first broadcast on ITV. >>

Shabby-genteel

At the inquest into Chapman's murder, Elizabeth Long described having seen Chapman standing outside 29 Hanbury Street at about 5:30 a.m. in the company of a dark-haired man wearing a brown deer-stalker hat and dark overcoat, and of a "shabby-genteel" appearance. [48]

Gau-Algesheim and Gau-Bickelheim

Together with Ockenheim and Gau-Algesheim, Gau-Bickelheim [until about the Congress of Vienna in 1814/15] formed the core of the Algesheim district. [49] These are the references between the places in the early modern period.

---

[48] https://en.wikipedia.org/wiki/Jack_the_Ripper
[49] https://www.regionalgeschichte.net/rheinhessen/gau-bickelheim.html

Peter Koser, pastor at that time

My first book in 2015 focused on the side of the Catholic Church in Mainz as well as the country parish priests in Gau-Bickelheim, because Anton Zahn served time in the penitentiary in Mainz in 1863-69. It is unclear whether it had an effect here.

My second book, 2021, then put a lot of emphasis on secular people, especially aristocrats who ruled the German Empire. The motif is also shown in this.

The 2 parties can perhaps be compared with the Mainz Cathedral, which has a secular (east) and a spiritual (west) side.

The parish priest at that time was Peter Koser. The internet states:

Peter Koser (* 14 December 1834 in Lampertheim; † 13 September 1891 in Darmstadt) was a Catholic priest and parish priest in Gau-Algesheim from 1869 to 1889.

Koser was ordained priest on 12 August 1859. He spent his years as chaplain in Gau-Bickelheim and Darmstadt. In 1866 he was appointed parish administrator of the parish of Wald-Michelbach and was then parish priest in Ober-Ingelheim for a short time. On 1 October 1869, the Bishop of Mainz, Wilhelm Emmanuel von Ketteler, entrusted Koser with the management of the parish of Gau-Algesheim, which had been looked after by a parish administrator for a long period of time, and which Koser held until 1889. From Gau-Algesheim he was transferred to Darmstadt to the parish of St. Ludwig, where he died on 13 September 1891. His body was transferred to Gau-Algesheim and buried in the parish church in the presence of the Bishop of Mainz. In 1894, a street adjoining the town centre was named "Koserstraße". [50]

Koser was chaplain in Gau-Bickelheim (around 1860), i.e. at the time when Anton Zahn was still living there at the age of about 20.
Perhaps Peter Koser knew the young man and also his character, which may already have been strange at that time. He is classified as "MAD" in the New York Sing Sing.

Koser became pastor of Gau-Algesheim exactly in 1869, when Anton Zahn was released from prison in Mainz and perhaps started working for the Avenarius company, which was founded in that year.

Koser and Avenarius know each other extremely well for understandable reasons. The one cultivates his Catholicism, the other is very much in favour of the National Liberals.

After all, Koser was a parish priest in Gau-Algesheim until 1889 and thus covered the autumn of 1888 in London and January 1889 in Managua in terms of time.

But an involvement in the Jack the Ripper action is not recognisable.

---

[50] https://de.wikipedia.org/wiki/Peter_Koser

Emil Schüller – OB Koblenz since 1888

Emil Schüller (* 11 January 1843 in Elberfeld, today a district of Wuppertal; † 8 May 1900 in Koblenz) was a German lawyer and Lord Mayor of Koblenz from 1888 to 1900. He was thus at the same time the representative of his city in the Prussian House of Lords.

Schüller was born the son of a notary public and studied law in Bonn and Heidelberg. In 1862 he became a corpsman of the Rhenania Bonn. He was first a justice of the peace in Velbert and then the first alderman of the city of Krefeld. Schüller was unanimously elected Lord Mayor of Koblenz by the Koblenz City Council and was inaugurated on 16 April 1888. On 25 October 1899 he was again unanimously re-elected for a second twelve-year term.
One year later, however, Schüller died of a heart attack at the age of 57. He was married to Karola Schüller née Bamberger (1871-1926). [51]

Here the name "Bamberger" comes up again. In my last book it was the Reichstag representative for Bingen-Alzey, Ludwig Bamberger.

I wonder if that plays a role in the selection of the conspirators.
Despite the 60 km from the 1888 house in Pfaffen-Schwabenheim to the Kaiserin-Augusta-Anlagen in Koblenz, no involvement can be proven for Emil Schüller.

---

[51] https://de.wikipedia.org/wiki/Emil_Schüller

Supplements

Wine hall of Köth in Pfaffen-Schwabenheim

The wine hall in Kreuznacher Straße, opposite the two stately villas of the Köth brothers, both wine merchants, looks like this: (Advertising etc. hidden)

It is also owned by the Köth brothers. Here you can see the dimensions of the wine business. Originally, the houses were to be more ornate on the façade. But they probably didn't want to snub the other rich winegrowers. The hall has roughly the same dimensions as the hall of the winegrowers' cooperative in Sprendlinger Straße. Pfaffen-Schwabenheim is probably also involved in the Jack-the-Ripper action. (See my books before). I only mention(ed) the wine merchants Köth to see what relations to the nobility and other influential persons are possible in 1888.

More from the 1888 house plan

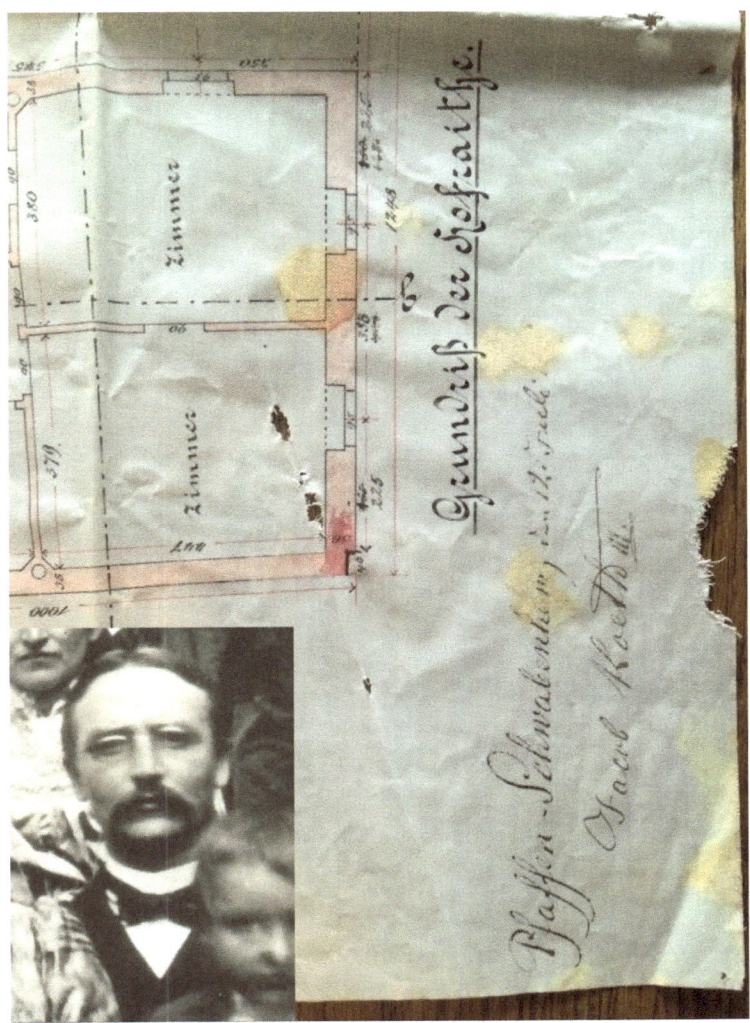

Pfaffen-Schwabenheim, 12. Juli [1888], Jacob Köth III.
Portrait: Jacob Köth III. (1850 - 1904) in the summer of 1903

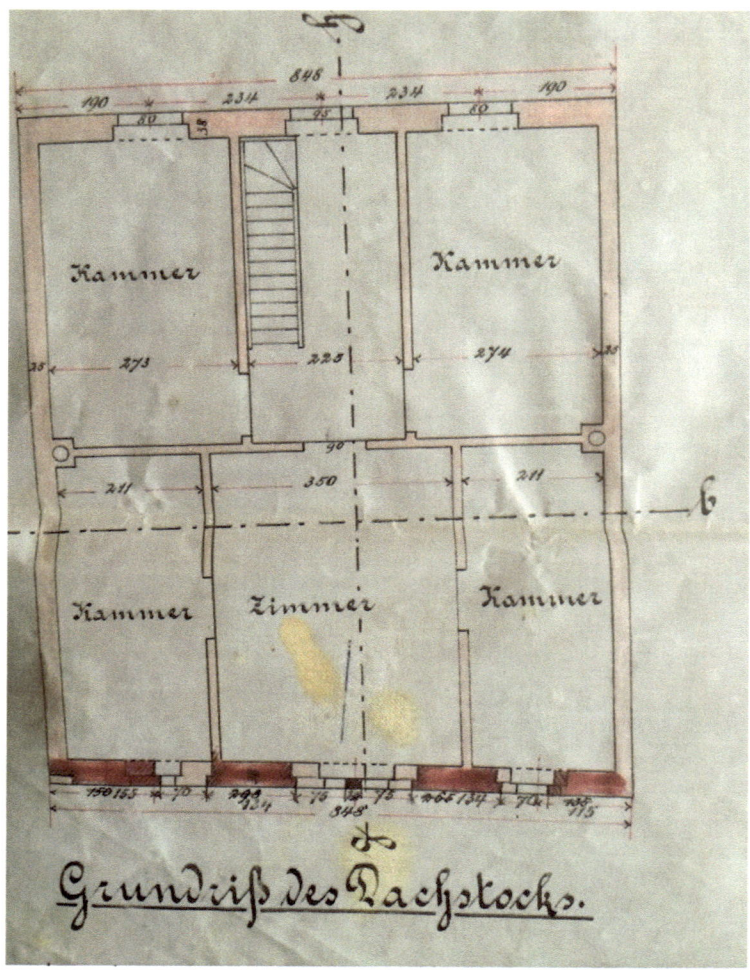

Grundriß des Dachstocks.

A son (living in Gau-Algesheim) of the Dittner couple visited us in Febr. 2022. I had visited his mother (+1974) and father (+1976) in 1970 in the 1888 house in Pfaffen-Schwabenheim together with my mother. He told me that the interior walls were plastered. The Niclas family, later in Mainz-Bretzenheim, previously lived in the house.

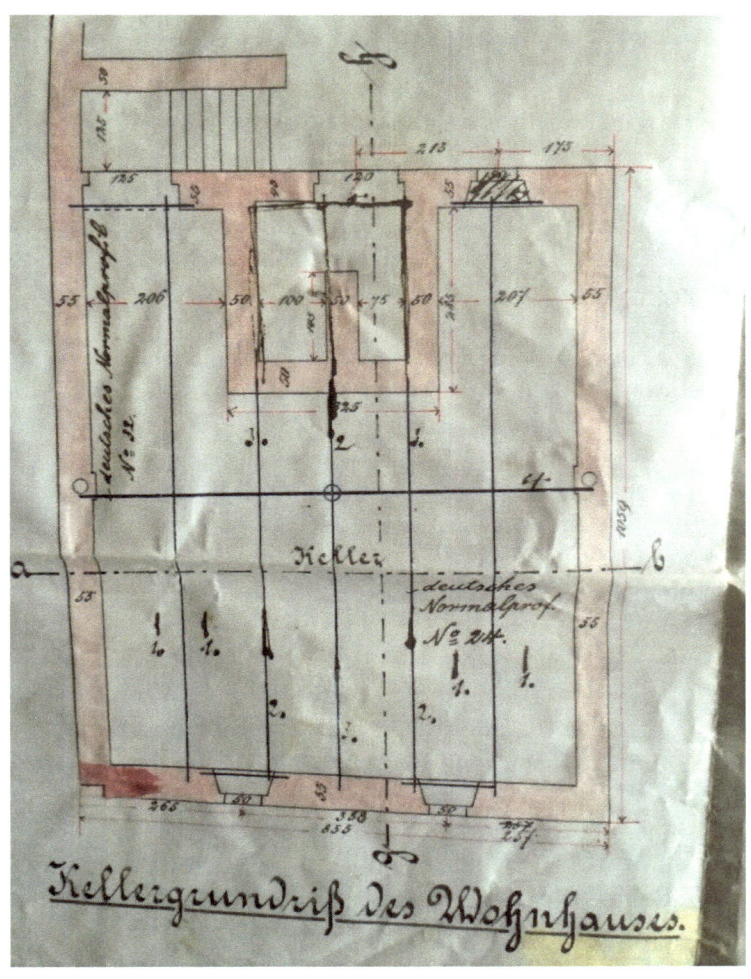

Kellergrundriß des Wohnhauses.

My cousin, who owns the 1888 house, married into Gau-Algesheim. So we have a reference here twice from Pfaffen-Schwabenheim and Gau-Algesheim. She told me that the staircase entrance was moved into the house. And not as on the plan.

Does Jacob Köth III. look like Albrecht Stosch?

Summary

Distances of the waters from Managua

This first of the three points in this book seems to me to be the most certain. The murder of the six women in Managua in Jack-the-Ripper style - and probably also carried out by the same person as in London 4 months earlier - is supposed to refer to the number "6".
The rear element of the name of the city and also of the state of Nicaragua, i.e. "Agua" (water) is supposed to be code for the waters in intervals of six.

If you take the central "Laguna" in Managua, there is another, smaller "Laguna" at a distance of 6 km, the Pacific Ocean in an exact southerly direction at a distance of a good 60 km and a lake in Guatemala at a distance of 600 km.

Google Maps, as we had seen in my last book, assumes a perfect earth level. Anything else would be too complicated for a detective of posterity. At the time, the trackers did not want to make this unnecessarily cumbersome.

At the same time, the Managua action in January 1889 is an invitation to try distance between Whitechapel and Gau-Bickelheim, where Anton Zahn alias Jack the Ripper comes from. And lo and behold! The detective in posterity gets exactly 600 km distance. (See my book: "Jack the Ripper - Deutscher vom Rhein", in English "Jack the Ripper - Codes lead to Germany")

6 km are between Gau-Bickelheim (cemetery) and the 1888 house in Pfaffen-Schwabenheim; 60 km from this house to the Krönungsweg in Frankfurt (cathedral, Römer) and to the south end of the Kaiserin-Augusta-Anlagen in Koblenz.

Even more amazing are the 6000 km from Managua!

Once you hit a lake in Canada, where the Yellowknife people (founded in 1930) live. Here the word "knife" is obvious.
And another time you reach a chain of lakes in Argentina at a distance of 6000 km, which from above looks like a knife pointed (towards the east).

These tracks are no coincidence, but have been laid on purpose, freely according to the motto: "Just see if it works. If it does, then we'll lay the track."

Codes in the name Carl Feigenbaum?

With all the many codes I had found in the last book (perhaps someone before me has noticed this), such as:

Buck's (Row), Hanbury (Street), Berner (St.), Mitre (Square).
= Herbert, Bismarck, neun (nine), bury (for example).

Nichols-Walker; Chapman-Smith; Stride-Gustafsdotter
= Hamilton-Douglas, Kaiser (emperor), verschwistert (related), nachts (at night)/nahmst (took) + rest / F=V (Gustafsdotter and Gustavsdotter)

I also had the idea to look for a code in the alias name "Carl Feigenbaum" of Anton Zahn because of the photo of the company Avenarius (1892).
However, the Spanish and English variants of the first name "Carl" must be used, which is not too far-fetched if one accepts the link with London and Managua in this German conspiracy.
(With the Pythagorean numerical code it is possible to form a word with "Carl" if the "a" becomes an "o").

a) Carlos Feigenbaum = Carbolineum + rest

b) Charles Feigenbaum = Gau-Algesheim + rest / C=G

c) Carlos/Charles Feigenbaum = Avenarius + rest / F =V

...thus

a) "Produced goods", b) "Place" and c) "Company name".

Together with the 1892 photo of the Avenarius company, where an employee looks something like Carl Feigenbaum (but is the height correct?) and the proximity to Gau-Bickelheim, Pfaffen-Schwabenheim and Horrweiler, perhaps a decoding could really be intended.

I would be happy to be proven wrong. If it is to be the system "company name, place, goods", then which other places, companies and goods come into question?

As written, the head of the company must not have known anything about the Jack the Ripper action. The only link to the nobility runs through his grandfather, who gave away Stolzenfels Castle to the later King of Prussia.

But that is no indication.

Carl Feigenbaum was probably already Anton Zahn's alias on the ships Reiher and Sperber from Bremerhaven to London in the autumn of 1888.

Photographie 1892 of Anton Zahn?

I would like to see experts or specialists here who would take a thorough look at this matter: Can the man in the photo in Gau-Algesheim at the Avenarius company in 1892 be the Carl Feigenbaum who was executed in the electric chair in New York State in 1896? Does he at least happen to look like him? **A lot of things seem to fit, but in the end it may fail because of the body height!**

If my assumption is disproved, I apologize to the person and indirectly to the company.

List of sources

-Google Maps (Function: measure distance)
-Various Wikipedia pages in German, English and Spanish (Retrieved early February 2022), Taken verbatim, please refer to Wikipedia for source information.
-Other internet pages, also given in footnotes (Retrieved early February 2022)
-Marriott, Trevor, Jack the Ripper: The 21st Century Investigation, Editor: John Blake; New Edition (30. April 2007) via Internet
-Hattemer, Thomas, Jack the Ripper – Verdächtigter vom Rhein, Books on Demand, 2015
-Hattemer, Thomas, Jack the Ripper – Deutscher vom Rhein, Books on Demand, 2021
-Hattemer, Thomas, Jack the Ripper – Codes lead to Germany, Books on Demand, 2021
-Universalatlas, Die Welt in Karten, RV-Verlag, Ostfildern, ISBN 3 575 02008 6

Translation

Translated with www.DeepL.com/Translator (free version)

List of illustrations

Jacob Köth III. (1850-1904), detail from photo 1903, private Used on page: 10 / overall photo used for the wedding of my great-grandparents Used on page: 43

Group picture of employees of the Avenarius Carbolineum company in Gau-Algesheim. The dates 1867 and 1892 are

written on barrels, certainly because of the 25th anniversary. Copies received in 2000 from Arnold Avenarius-Herborn, Gau-Algesheim
Used on pages: 56 (photographed too small in 2000), 61 (rough paper copy)

Detail of the group picture 1892 at the Avenarius company with probably the oldest employee, who might be Anton Zahn (1841 - 1896). Upper, back row, 4th person from left.
Used on pages: 48, 50, 62 (right)

Detail of the group picture 1892 at the Avenarius company with one barrel and its inscription,
Used on page: 71

Carl Ferdinand Feigenbaum (actually: Anton Zahn) (1841-1896), file "zahn10.jpg", graphic from website https://victorianripper.forumotion.com/t1884-fiegenbaum-was-an.alias, comment above the graphic: "By telegraph to the Herald", graphic uploaded by "Karen".
Used on page: 62 (left)

Albert Fish (b. 19 May 1870 in Washington, D.C. as Hamilton Howard Fish; † 16 January 1936 in Sing Sing, Ossining), file: "Albert Fish 1903.JPG", Taken from: https://commons.wikimedia.org/wiki/File:Albert_Fish_1903.JPG; Licence: work "public domain" (English) Source: http://www.nydailynews.com/new-york/1928-murder-grace-budd-albert-fish-gallery-1.1277430?pmSlide=10
Used on page: 64

Johann Otto Hoch (actually: Johann Schmitt/Schmidt) (1855-1906), File: "Johann Otto Hoch.jpg", photo before 1906, photographer unknown, detail,
Taken from: https://commons.m.wikimedia.org

Johann Otto Hoch (actually: Johann Schmitt/Schmidt)
Here is Johann Hoch, considered the peer of Bluebeards,
who died on the gallows in Chicago in 1906 after he had
been found guilty of killing twelve "wives".
https://murderpedia.org/male.H/h/hoch-johann-
photos.htm
Used on page: 65 (right)

Köth wine hall opposite the two mansions and next to the
former tramway diversion station (1908 - 1960s),
Kreuznacher Straße, Pfaffen-Schwabenheim, photograph
taken in November 2021, private.
Used on page: 78

Three cut-outs from the building plan of the 1888 house at
Kreuznacher Straße 31, Pfaffen-Schwabenheim, private
property from the estate of my grandparents Karl Kolb II.
(1899-1987) and Anna Elisabeth née Diegel (1904-1956),
who had inherited the house and rented it out.
Used on the pages: 79, 80, 81

Jakob Koeth (1850-1904), detail of the photograph
celebrating the wedding of my great-grandparents
Heinrich Diegel IV and Helena née Wetzel on the farm;
summer 1903. (Private property)
Used on page: 79

When I visited London with my parents and brother in 1980, I could not have guessed that on my mother's side I was apparently so strongly connected with a part of the city's history. We were on our way to visit acquaintances in Nafferton (Yorkshire), who came from Transylvania and the Palatinate, to make a round trip through Scotland.

I also have connections with London on my father's side: My father's cousin from Mainz married a diplomat who had been German ambassador to Norway from 1992 to 1996 and envoy, i.e. deputy ambassador, to London from 1988 to 1992. In this capacity, Helmut Wegner (1931 - 2019) had the task of organising the closure of the GDR embassy.

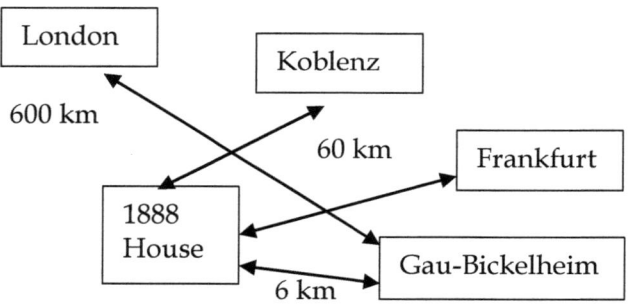

Dedicated to my father Peter, civil engineer
20.03.1940 - 20.02.2022 and
to my mother Liane
26.09.1943 - 12.03.2022
Both died in Pfaffen-Schwabenheim

Thomas Hattemer, born in Bad Kreuznach in 1967, grew up in Pfaffen-Schwabenheim, graduated in physics in Mainz in 1994.